SUCCESS MNSTR™
WORKBOOK

SUCCESS MNSTR™ WORKBOOK

Ashley Armstrong

Paperback ISBN: 978-1-965653-20-3

DISCLAIMER

Read This First...

Welcome!

You've likely already purchased *Success MNSTR: Conquering Unseen Challenges as You Strive to Reach Your Goals* (and if not, go grab it now on Amazon).

This accompanying workbook is designed to help you dive deeper into each chapter, review what you've read, and capture your insights and epiphanies along the way. For easy access to all the tools and resources in the MNSTR Universe, here's the resource page again.

Scan with your cell phone or type in the URL:

www.successmnstr.com/resources

Contents

Introduction

Success MNSTR™ Workbook Overview

The *Success MNSTR™ Workbook* is a practical companion to *Success MNSTR™: Conquering Unseen Challenges as You Strive to Reach Your Goals,* offering exercises, self-reflection questions, and actionable activities. Designed for high achievers, it helps users identify their unique Success MNSTR Archetype, manage the emotional highs and lows of success, and apply the MNSTR Technique to real-life situations.

Key Features:

- **Self-Assessment Tools:** Identify behavior patterns, emotional triggers, and cycles of self-sabotage while uncovering your Success MNSTR Archetype.

- **Actionable Activities:** Engage with fill-in-the-blanks, writing prompts, and matching exercises to apply the MNSTR Technique and track your progress.

- **Questions & Answer Key:** Each chapter includes questions and answers to reinforce key concepts and promote critical thinking.

- **Writing Prompts:** Reflect on your success journey and personal growth through targeted prompts.

- **Goal-Oriented Exercises:** Set actionable goals and track them while maintaining balance in your personal and professional life.

- **MNSTR Technique™ Implementation:** Use a step-by-step guide to evaluate your mindset, emotions, and goals, and take corrective actions.

- **Progress Reviews:** Regularly track your growth, set new goals, and realign with your objectives.

How to Use the Workbook

This workbook is designed to accompany the *Success MNSTR™: Conquering Unseen Challenges as You Strive to Reach Your Goals* book, providing deeper insights into each chapter. As you work through the book, refer to the workbook to:

- Reflect on key lessons.

- Complete exercises to strengthen understanding.

- Track your emotional and psychological growth.

- Implement the MNSTR Technique in daily life.

- Record your insights, challenges, and achievements.

Regular engagement with the workbook will build resilience, increase self-awareness, and help you develop a personalized strategy for lasting success. It is a valuable tool to stay aligned with your goals and avoid emotional burnout, whether you're beginning your journey or already excelling.

Chapter 1
Introduction & Success

1. Related Questions with an Answer Key:

Question 1: What common belief about success is challenged in the chapter?

_____

_____

_____

_____

Answer: The chapter challenges the belief that understanding success comes only after achieving it. It suggests that learning about success should begin before reaching arbitrary milestones.

Question 2: How does the chapter describe the post-success experience of high achievers?

_____

_____

_____

_____

Answer: The chapter describes the post-success experience as potentially overwhelming and even nightmarish, bringing about new expectations, pressures, and the risk of burnout.

Question 3: What methodology is introduced in the chapter to help high achievers?

_____

_____

_____

_____

Answer: The Success MNSTR™ methodology is introduced, which includes identifying one's Success MNSTR Archetype and applying the five key elements of the MNSTR Technique™.

Question 4: According to the chapter, what are some tangible benefits high achievers enjoy?

_____

_____

_____

_____

Answer: High achievers enjoy tangible benefits such as financial freedom, the ability to hire help, and opportunities for fun and philanthropy.

Question 5: What are some intangible rewards that high achievers seek, as defined in the chapter?

_____

_____

_____

_____

Answer: Intangible rewards include personal growth, self-awareness, the joy of the process, and authentic success encompassing mental and physical well-being and meaningful relationships.

2. Multiple Choice Questions:

Question 1: According to the chapter, when should one start learning about success?

    a) After achieving it

    b) Once they are wealthy

    c) As soon as they enter the workforce

    d) Before reaching any arbitrary milestone

Answer: d) Before reaching any arbitrary milestone

Question 2: What emotion did the author feel upon hitting a major milestone of success?

    a) Pure joy

    b) Confusion

    c) Initially exhilarated, then overwhelmed

    d) Complete indifference

Answer: c) Initially exhilarated, then overwhelmed

Question 3: Which of the following is NOT listed as a characteristic of high achievers?

    a) Unyielding passion

    b) Complacency

    c) Goal-oriented approaches

    d) Resilience in the face of adversity

Answer: b) Complacency

Question 4: What is the dual nature of success as discussed in the chapter?

    a) It brings wealth but not happiness

    b) It is exhilarating but can lead to burnout

    c) It is lonely but makes one independent

    d) It is elusive yet attainable

Answer: b) It is exhilarating but can lead to burnout

Question 5: High achievers often redefine success to include which of the following?

    a) Wealth only

    b) Personal growth and self-awareness

    c) Recognition from peers

    d) Avoidance of risks

Answer: b) Personal growth and self-awareness

3. Topical Writing Prompts:

Reflect on a time when you felt successful. What were the immediate emotions and the subsequent challenges you faced?

_____

_____

_____

_____

_____

_____

_____

_____

_____

_____

_____

Discuss how society's narrow definitions of success can impact one's personal fulfillment and sense of identity.

_____

_____

_____

_____

_____

_____

_____

_____

_____

Write about the relationship between resilience and success. Why is resilience particularly vital for high achievers?

_____

_____

_____

_____

_____

_____

_____

_____

_____

Consider the benefits and drawbacks of being a high achiever. How can one manage the pressures to maintain a healthy balance?

_____

_____

_____

_____

_____

_____

_____

_____

_____

Explore the concept of redefining success. What does "holistic success" mean to you personally, and how can it be achieved?

_____

_____

_____

_____

_____

_____

_____

_____

_____

_____

_____

_____

_____

4. Additional Workbook Activities:

Matching Exercise:

Match the following terms with their definitions:

    a) Unyielding Passion

    b) Resilience

    c) Proactive Mindset

    d) Personal Fulfillment

    e) Burnout

Definitions:

    1. Physical and mental exhaustion due to relentless drive and commitment.

    2. Satisfaction and sense of purpose from achieving goals.

    3. Creating opportunities rather than waiting for them.

    4. The ability to bounce back from failures and emerge stronger.

    5. A deep-seated commitment that fuels a high achiever's journey.

Answer: a-5, b-4, c-3, d-2, e-1,

Fill-in-the-Blanks:

Complete the sentences with the correct words:

1. High achievers possess a(n) _____ passion for their chosen fields.
2. The chapter introduces the Success MNSTR™ methodology to assist high achievers by identifying their _____.
3. One must start understanding success _____ reaching any significant milestone.
4. Success is not just about wealth but also about experiencing _____ growth and self-awareness.
5. High achievers often struggle with feelings of _____ despite their accomplishments.

Answer: unyielding, Success MNSTR Archetype, before, unworthiness

Discussion Topics:

Discuss the following topics in groups or pairs:

How does society's definition of success compare to your personal definition?

_____

_____

_____

_____

_____

What are some strategies high achievers can use to manage burnout and maintain balance?

_____

_____

_____

_____

Debate whether success is more impactful when measured by tangible outcomes or intrinsic satisfaction.

_____

_____

_____

_____

Share personal experiences where your own goals clashed with societal expectations of success.

_____

_____

_____

_____

_____

Discuss how recognizing one's Success MNSTR Archetype could be beneficial in pursuing sustainable success.

_____

_____

_____

_____

_____

What surprised you?

_____

_____

_____

_____

_____

_____

_____

What upset you?

_____

_____

_____

_____

_____

_____

_____

What was your biggest takeaway?

_____

_____

_____

_____

_____

_____

_____

Anything else worth noting:

_____

_____

_____

_____

_____

_____

_____

_____

What key takeaway will you highlight when you share this on social media (#SuccessMNSTR)?

_____

_____

_____

_____

_____

_____

_____

_____

P.S. Email the link to your post to Hello@SuccessMNSTR.com for an extra bonus!

Chapter 2
Bridging the Gap Between Generic Success Principles and Custom Strategies

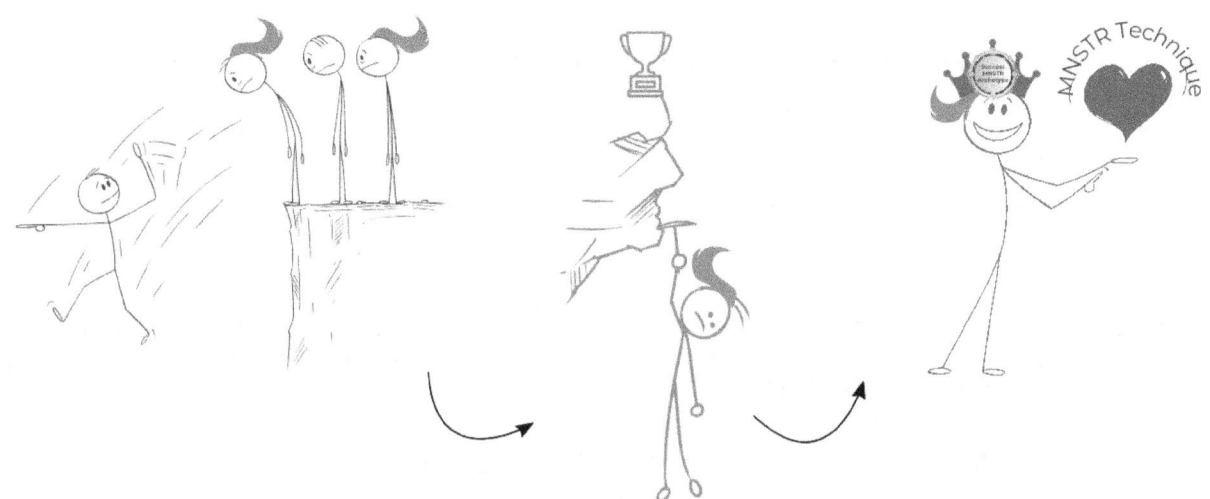

1. Related Questions with an Answer Key:

Question 1: What role do generic success principles play in personal and professional growth?

_____

_____

_____

Answer: Generic success principles provide a broad foundation, offering tools and guidelines that can help individuals pursue personal and professional growth.

Question 2: Why do high achievers need more than basic success strategies?

_____

_____

_____

Answer: High achievers need more than basic strategies because they operate in realms defined by unique challenges and lofty ambitions, where conventional advice might fall short.

Question 3: What are some of the deeper questions high achievers might confront?

_____

_____

_____

_____

Answer: High achievers might confront deeper questions such as "Was it just luck?", "Do I really need to keep putting myself out there?", and "How can I keep going without burning out?", "Now what?"

Question 4: Describe the personal journey that led to the creation of the Success MNSTR Archetypes and the MNSTR Technique.

_____

_____

_____

_____

Answer: The author describes a personal journey filled with high expectations, achievement, and subsequent emotional turmoil. This led to the introspection and study of neuroscience, psychology, and personality traits that resulted in the creation of the Success MNSTR Archetypes and the MNSTR Technique.

Question 5: What is the main purpose of the MNSTR Technique?

_____

_____

_____

_____

Answer: The MNSTR Technique is designed to help high achievers manage the emotional highs and lows of achievement, recognize destructive patterns, and navigate their paths with clarity and purpose.

2. Multiple Choice Questions:

Question 1: What is the main argument presented in this chapter?

    a) Success is solely defined by external achievements

    b) Success is not a "One Size Fits All" model

    c) High achievers do not face unique challenges

    d) Generic success principles are irrelevant

Answer: b) Success is not a "One Size Fits All" model

Question 2: What emotional challenges do high achievers often face?

a) Complacency

b) Overconfidence

c) Burnout and self-doubt

d) Lack of ambition

Answer: c) Burnout and self-doubt

Question 3: Why did the author move across the country and abroad?

a) To take a vacation

b) To explore new sports

c) To prove herself and seek new opportunities

d) To visit family

Answer: c) To prove herself and seek new opportunities

Question 4: What realization marked a turning point for the author?

a) Generic success principles were enough

b) Material wealth guarantees happiness

c) She was stuck in an endless cycle of chasing success

d) She did not need to achieve anymore

Answer: c) She was stuck in an endless cycle of chasing success

Question 5: What is the ultimate goal of the MNSTR Technique?

a) To help high achievers become wealthy

b) To ensure high achievers keep chasing new goals

c) To help high achievers find clarity and purpose beyond just checking off goals

d) To eliminate competition

Answer: c) To help high achievers find clarity and purpose beyond just checking off goals

3. Topical Writing Prompts:

Discuss how the pressure to achieve can impact one's mental and emotional health.

_____

_____

_____

_____

_____

_____

_____

_____

Reflect on a time when you felt the emotional highs and lows of success. How did you cope with it?

_____

_____

_____

_____

_____

_____

_____

How can personalized strategies better support high achievers in managing the emotional impact of success?

_____

_____

_____

_____

_____

_____

_____

Explain how the author's background influenced her outlook on success and failure.

_____

_____

_____

_____

_____

_____

_____

Analyze the concept of the Success MNSTR and how it can affect one's approach to personal and professional life.

_____

_____

_____

_____

_____

_____

_____

_____

4. Additional Workbook Activities:

Matching Exercise:

Match the following terms with their definitions:
- a) Success MNSTR
- b) MNSTR Technique
- c) Burnout
- d) Self-Doubt
- e) High Achievers

Definitions:

- i) A concept representing the negative side effects of achievement.
- ii) A structured method to manage the emotional highs and lows of success.
- iii) A state of emotional, physical, and mental exhaustion caused by excessive and prolonged stress.
- iv) A lack of confidence in one's own abilities or actions.
- v) Individuals who set and accomplish ambitious goals and face unique challenges.

Answers: a-i, b-ii, c-iii, d-iv, e-v

Fill-in-the-Blanks:

Complete the sentences with the correct words:

1. High achievers often need more than _____ strategies to support their unique challenges.
2. The _____ MNSTR represents the negative emotional patterns associated with constant achievement.
3. Personalized strategies can help manage burnout and _____.
4. The author's realization came from a pattern observed during periods of high _____ and subsequent emotional turmoil.
5. The MNSTR Technique helps in navigating the highs and lows of achievement without losing one's _____.

Answers: advanced, Success, self-doubt, achievement, purpose

Discussion Topics:

Discuss the following topics in groups or pairs:

The impact of family expectations on personal achievement.

_____

_____

_____

_____

_____

Strategies to balance professional success with personal well-being.

_____

_____

_____

_____

_____

How can high achievers maintain motivation without burning out?

_____

_____

_____

_____

_____

The role of self-awareness and introspection in managing success.

_____

_____

_____

_____

_____

Compare and contrast generic success principles with personalized strategies.

_____
_____
_____
_____
_____

What surprised you?

_____
_____
_____
_____
_____
_____
_____
_____

What upset you?

_____
_____
_____
_____
_____
_____
_____
_____

What was your biggest takeaway?

_____
_____
_____
_____
_____
_____
_____

Anything else worth noting:

_____

_____

_____

_____

_____

_____

_____

_____

_____

What key takeaway will you highlight when you share this on social media (#SuccessMNSTR)?

_____

_____

_____

_____

_____

_____

_____

_____

_____

P.S. Email the link to your post to Hello@SuccessMNSTR.com for an extra bonus!

Chapter 3
The Success MNSTR Archetypes

What is your Success MNSTR Archetype?

Take 5 minutes now to complete the quiz if you haven't already. Simply scan the QR code with your phone or type the URL into your browser.

www.successmnstr.com/resources

POLITICIAN: Y / N

How do you feel about it?

_____

_____

_____

_____

_____

_____

MONARCH: Y / N

How do you feel about it?

_____

_____

_____

_____

_____

_____

ATHLETE: Y / N

How do you feel about it?

_____

_____

_____

_____

_____

_____

PUBLIC ADVOCATE: Y / N

How do you feel about it?

_____

_____

_____

_____

_____

_____

ENTREPRENEUR: Y / N

How do you feel about it?

_____

_____

_____

_____

_____

_____

SCIENTIST: Y / N

How do you feel about it?

_____

_____

_____

_____

_____

_____

GLOBAL NOMAD: Y / N

How do you feel about it?

_____

_____

_____

_____

_____

_____

INFLUENCER: Y / N

How do you feel about it?

_____

_____

_____

_____

_____

_____

EDUCATED: Y / N

How do you feel about it?

_____

_____

_____

_____

_____

_____

After reading the book, do you resonate with more than one archetype? If yes, why?

_____

_____

_____

_____

(That's perfectly normal, by the way! Humans are multi-faceted creatures who shift and evolve as we experience life.)

1. Related Questions with an Answer Key:

Question 1: What is the primary purpose of identifying your Success MNSTR Archetype according to the chapter?

_____

_____

_____

Answer: Identifying your Success MNSTR Archetype provides self-discovery and insights into your strengths, motivations, and potential challenges, which helps in personal growth and navigating the journey toward success effectively.

Question 2: Describe the main motivations that drive the Athlete Archetype.

_____

_____

_____

Answer: The Athlete is driven by a profound passion for excelling in their chosen field, the exhilaration of competition, the pursuit of victory, and the thirst for recognition and admiration.

Question 3: What are some of the supportive strengths and behaviors associated with the Influencer Archetype?

_____

_____

_____

_____

Answer: The Influencer possesses natural charisma, skills in self-promotion, networking, and personal branding, as well as resilience, effective communication, adaptability, and creativity.

Question 4: What is the Treadmill Trap for the Scientist Archetype?

_____

_____

_____

_____

Answer: The Treadmill Trap for Scientists involves seeking constant recognition and validation, which can lead to complacency and risk avoidance that prevents true innovation.

Question 5: How can sharing your Success MNSTR Archetype on social media benefit you?

_____

_____

_____

_____

Answer: Sharing your Success MNSTR Archetype on social media fosters a sense of community and connection, reminding you that others face similar challenges and triumphs, which can be empowering and supportive.

2. Multiple Choice Questions:

Question 1: What is a significant aspect of the Athlete's motivation?

a) The desire for financial independence

b) The thrill of competition and victory

c) The need for knowledge

d) The quest for social justice

Answer: b) The thrill of competition and victory

Question 2: Which of the following is not a sabotaging dark side of the Influencer?

a) Seeking external validation excessively

b) An unhealthy obsession with perfection

c) Pressure to curate a perfect public image

d) Negative feedback straining mental health

Answer: b) An unhealthy obsession with perfection

Question 3: What is a strength of the Entrepreneur Archetype?

a) Emotional detachment in problem-solving

b) Expertise in building symbiotic relationships

c) Passion for innovation and financial acumen

d) Aptitude for efficient communication and networking

Answer: c) Passion for innovation and financial acumen

Question 4: Which archetype is driven by the pursuit of knowledge and peer recognition?

a) Athlete

b) Influencer

c) Scientist

d) Global Nomad

Answer: c) Scientist

Question 5: What is a common challenge faced by the Monarch Archetype?

a) An incessant need for constant validation

b) A tendency to alienate those with less knowledge

c) An obsession with maintaining control

d) Fear of failure and self-doubt

Answer: c) An obsession with maintaining control

3. Topical Writing Prompts:

Reflect on a time when you identified with one of the Success MNSTR Archetypes. How did this insight help you overcome a challenge?

_____

_____

_____

_____

_____

_____

_____

_____

_____

_____

_____

How can understanding your Success MNSTR Archetype contribute to personal and professional growth?

_____

_____

_____

_____

_____

_____

_____

_____

_____

Discuss the potential dark sides of your identified archetype and strategies to manage them.

_____

_____

_____

_____

_____

_____

_____

_____

_____

Describe how sharing your archetype on social media could foster a sense of community and support.

_____

_____

_____

_____

_____

_____

_____

_____

Explore how different archetypes might collaborate effectively in a team setting.

_____

_____

_____

_____

_____

_____

_____

_____

_____

4. Additional Workbook Activities:

Matching Exercise:

Match the following Success MNSTR Archetypes with their primary motivation.

    a) Athlete

    b) Influencer

    c) Scientist

    d) Entrepreneur

    e) Public Advocate

Motivation:

    1. The thrill of competition and recognition

    2. Popularity, recognition, and validation

    3. Pursuit of knowledge and solving complex problems

    4. Desire for financial control and autonomy

    5. Desire for meaningful change and social justice

Answer: a-1, b-2, c-3, d-4, e-5

Fill-in-the-Blanks:

Complete the sentences with the concepts from the chapter:

    1. The Athlete Archetype is driven by the pursuit of _____ and the thrill of _____.

    2. The Influencer emphasizes _____ and building a _____ public image.

    3. The Scientist values _____ and strives for _____ in their work.

    4. Entrepreneurs are motivated by the drive for financial _____ and taking _____.

    5. Public Advocates focus on creating _____ change and advocating for _____.

Answer: excellence; competition, networking; perfect, knowledge; accuracy, control; risks, social; justice

Discussion Topics:

Discuss the following topics in groups or pairs:

How can identifying your Success MNSTR Archetype impact your long-term goals?

_____

_____

_____

_____

_____

What strategies can be implemented to avoid the Treadmill Trap associated with your archetype?

_____

_____

_____

_____

_____

How does knowing your archetype help in overcoming personal and professional obstacles?

_____

_____

_____

_____

_____

In what ways can understanding diverse archetypes improve teamwork and collaboration?

_____

_____

_____

_____

_____

How can the insights from your archetype quiz results align your aspirations and values?

_____

_____

_____

_____

What surprised you?

_____
_____
_____
_____
_____
_____
_____
_____

What upset you?

_____
_____
_____
_____
_____
_____
_____
_____

What was your biggest takeaway?

_____
_____
_____
_____
_____
_____
_____
_____

Anything else worth noting:

_____

_____

_____

_____

_____

_____

_____

_____

What key takeaway will you highlight when you share this on social media (#SuccessMNSTR)?

_____

_____

_____

_____

_____

_____

_____

_____

P.S. Email the link to your post to Hello@SuccessMNSTR.com for an extra bonus!

Chapter 4
Rewiring for Success: The MNSTR Technique

1. Related Questions with an Answer Key:

Question 1: What is the primary objective of Step #2 in the MNSTR Technique?

_____

_____

_____

_____

Answer: The primary objective of Step #2 is to enhance mindset, challenge societal expectations, build strong support systems, and set realistic goals that align with one's Success MNSTR Archetype.

Question 2: How does the orbitofrontal cortex (OFC) influence decision-making and habit formation?

_____

_____

_____

_____

Answer: The OFC plays a key role in decision-making and habit formation. When it's less active, people rely more on habits. When it's more active, they take time to think through choices more carefully.

Question 3: What percentage of everyday actions are done out of habit, according to Dr. Wendy Wood?

_____

_____

_____

_____

Answer: According to Dr. Wendy Wood, 43% of everyday actions are done out of habit while people think about other things.

Question 4: What is the "false hope syndrome" and how can it impact goal-setting?

_____

_____

_____

_____

Answer: The "false hope syndrome" occurs when people set unrealistic goals and underestimate the effort needed, overestimating the benefits and expecting quick results. Failure leads to another unrealistic attempt, creating a cycle of disappointment and misplaced confidence.

Question 5: What societal and mental health challenges are prevalent among high achievers?

_____

_____

_____

_____

Answer: High achievers often face burnout, imposter syndrome, prolonged work hours, and pressure to excel continuously, leading to mental health issues like anxiety and depression.

2. Multiple Choice Questions:

Question 1: What role does the MNSTR Technique play in stress management?

    a) Ignoring stressors

    b) Enhancing awareness of physical reactions and mental focus

    c) Encouraging avoidance of responsibilities

    d) Promoting multitasking

Answer: b) Enhancing awareness of physical reactions and mental focus

Question 2: According to the chapter, what percentage of working-age adults had a mental disorder in 2019?

    a) 10%

    b) 15%

    c) 20%

    d) 25%

Answer: b) 15%

Question 3: How does changing the location or routine help in habit formation?

    a) Makes the habit stronger

    b) Creates new triggers

    c) Diminishes the habit completely

    d) Causes unnecessary stress

Answer: b) Creates new triggers

Question 4: Who found that 43% of everyday actions are done out of habit?

    a) Dr. Wendy Wood

    b) Dr. Peter Herman

    c) Dr. Arthur Brooks

    d) Dr. Janet Polivy

Answer: a) Dr. Wendy Wood

Question 5: What aspect of brain function does the MNSTR Technique particularly leverage for habit management?

    a) Amygdala's emotional response

    b) Hippocampus's memory load

    c) Prefrontal cortex's decision-making process

    d) Brainstem's automatic functions

Answer: c) Prefrontal cortex's decision-making process

3. Topical Writing Prompts:

Discuss how the MNSTR Technique can help in overcoming imposter syndrome. Provide personalized strategies that you would adopt.

_____

_____

_____

_____

_____

_____

_____

_____

_____

_____

_____

Reflect on a personal experience where societal pressure impacted your mental well-being. How can the MNSTR Technique address such pressures?

_____

_____

_____

_____

_____

_____

_____

Analyze how "false hope syndrome" might have affected your previous goal-setting efforts and how you can rectify it using the MNSTR Technique.

_____

_____

_____

_____

_____

_____

Consider a habit you wish to change. Describe a step-by-step plan using insights from the chapter.

_____

_____

_____

_____

_____

_____

Explore the paradox of success in your life. How can understanding this paradox improve your approach to achievements?

_____

_____

_____

_____

_____

_____

4. Additional Workbook Activities:

Matching Exercise:

Match the following terms with their definitions:

    a) Orbitofrontal Cortex (OFC)

    b) False Hope Syndrome

    c) Success Depression

    d) Habit

    e) MNSTR Technique

Definitions:

    1. Part of the prefrontal cortex responsible for decision-making and habit formation.

    2. Setting unrealistic goals and underestimating the effort needed for success.

    3. Feeling of emptiness or sadness after achieving major goals.

    4. Behavior performed automatically due to repetition.

    5. Framework to manage stress, emotions, and mental health for high achievers.

Answers: a-1, b-2, c-3, d-4, d-5,

Fill-in-the-Blanks:

Complete the sentences with the correct words:

1. The orbitofrontal cortex (OFC) is crucial for balancing _____ behaviors and thoughtful decision-making.
2. According to Dr. Wendy Wood, _____ of everyday actions are done out of habit.
3. The "false hope syndrome" describes setting _____ and the resulting disappointment.
4. Changing _____ can help disrupt entrenched habits.
5. Even high income doesn't guarantee _____, as shown by the Marist Institute survey.

Answer: automatic, 43%, unrealistic goals, routine or location, happiness

Discussion Topics:

Discuss the following topics in groups or pairs:

How can the MNSTR Technique be applied in educational settings to manage stress and build resilience among students?

_____

_____

_____

_____

_____

Debate the impact of societal expectations on individual mental health and the ways to counter these pressures.

_____

_____

_____

_____

_____

Examine the role of the workplace in reducing career-related burnout and promoting mental well-being.

_____

_____

_____

_____

_____

Discuss the effectiveness of adding small actions to existing routines in forming new habits.

_____

_____

_____

_____

How can recognizing the signs of the "false hope syndrome" improve personal and professional goal-setting strategies?

_____

_____

_____

_____

_____

What surprised you?

_____

_____

_____

_____

_____

_____

What upset you?

_____

_____

_____

_____

_____

_____

What was your biggest takeaway?

_____
_____
_____
_____
_____
_____
_____

Anything else worth noting:

_____
_____
_____
_____
_____
_____
_____
_____

What key takeaway will you highlight when you share this on social media (#SuccessMNSTR)?

_____
_____
_____
_____
_____
_____
_____

P.S. Email the link to your post to Hello@SuccessMNSTR.com for an extra bonus!

Chapter 5
"M Stands for Mindset"

1. Related Questions with an Answer Key:

Question 1: What is a growth mindset, according to Dr. Carol Dweck's work?

_____

_____

_____

_____

Answer: A growth mindset is the belief that abilities can improve with effort and persistence.

Question 2: How did Thomas Edison exemplify a growth mindset?

_____

_____

_____

_____

Answer: Thomas Edison exemplified a growth mindset by viewing his thousands of failures as learning opportunities, ultimately leading to his breakthrough invention of the light bulb.

Question 3: What are the benefits of having a growth mindset for high achievers?

_____

_____

_____

_____

Answer: High achievers with a growth mindset are resilient in setbacks, adaptable to changing environments, eager to learn and improve, and view failures as growth opportunities.

Question 4: Why is cultivating a beginner's mindset important?

_____

_____

_____

_____

Answer: Cultivating a beginner's mindset is important because it helps maintain curiosity and openness, allowing individuals to see things from fresh perspectives and continuously learn.

Question 5: How can one shift their perspective on obstacles?

_____

_____

_____

_____

Answer: One can shift their perspective on obstacles by viewing them as opportunities for growth rather than as barriers, and by focusing on finding solutions rather than dwelling on challenges.

2. Multiple Choice Questions:

Question 1: What is the first step to a growth mindset?

    a) Embrace failure

    b) Cultivate a beginner's mindset

    c) Focus on increasing self-awareness

    d) Practice gratitude

Answer: c) Focus on increasing self-awareness

Question 2: According to the chapter, when is the best time for a power nap?

    a) 7:00 AM - 8:00 AM

    b) 10:00 AM - 11:00 AM

    c) 1:00 PM - 3:00 PM

    d) 4:00 PM - 5:00 PM

Answer: c) 1:00 PM - 3:00 PM

Question 3: How can one cultivate a gratitude mindset?

a) By focusing on failures

b) By reflecting daily on life's blessings and lessons

c) By being critical of oneself

d) By avoiding new experiences

Answer: b) By reflecting daily on life's blessings and lessons

Question 4: Why is it helpful to be intentional with your physical environment?

a) It creates distraction

b) It reduces productivity

c) It enhances concentration and mood

d) It increases screen time

Answer: c) It enhances concentration and mood

Question 5: What does "curating inspirational media" entail?

a) Watching the news frequently

b) Avoiding motivational content

c) Consuming positive content that fosters growth

d) Unfollowing positive influencers

Answer: c) Consuming positive content that fosters growth

3. Topical Writing Prompts:

Reflect on a recent failure and describe how viewing it with a growth mindset could change your perspective on it.

_____
_____
_____
_____
_____
_____
_____
_____
_____
_____
_____

Describe a situation where you had to step out of your comfort zone. How did this experience contribute to your personal growth?

_____

_____

_____

_____

_____

_____

_____

Explain how cultivating a beginner's mindset can impact your daily life and interactions with others.

_____

_____

_____

_____

_____

_____

_____

_____

Discuss the importance of choosing your peers consciously and how they can influence your growth mindset.

_____

_____

_____

_____

_____

_____

_____

Write about a time when gratitude helped you overcome a challenging situation.

_____

_____

_____

_____

_____

_____

_____

_____

4. Additional Workbook Activities:

Matching Exercise:

Match the following terms with their definitions:

    a) Growth Mindset

    b) Fixed Mindset

    c) Beginner's Mindset

    d) Power Naps

    e) Gratitude Mindset

Definitions:

    1. The belief that abilities can improve with effort and persistence.

    2. The belief that abilities are unchangeable.

    3. A mindset characterized by curiosity and openness.

    4. Short naps that enhance cognitive function and memory.

    5. Reflecting daily on life's blessings and lessons.

Answer: a-1, b-2, c-3, d-4, e-5

Fill-in-the-Blanks:

Complete the sentences with the correct words:

    1. A _____ mindset believes that abilities can improve with effort and persistence.

    2. A fixed mindset views setbacks as _____ rather than learning opportunities.

    3. _____ daily on life's blessings can help build a positive outlook.

    4. Surrounding oneself with peers committed to personal _____ promotes development.

    5. Taking power naps between _____ and _____ can boost cognitive functions.

Answer: growth, failures, Reflecting, growth, 1:00 PM, 3:00 PM

Discussion Topics:

Discuss the following topics in groups or pairs:

How can adopting a growth mindset impact your professional and personal life?

_____

_____

_____

_____

_____

What are some ways to cultivate a beginner's mindset in everyday activities?

_____

_____

_____

_____

_____

How can failure be used as a constructive feedback mechanism for achieving success?

_____

_____

_____

_____

_____

In what ways can your physical environment influence your productivity and mindset?

_____

_____

_____

_____

_____

What strategies can you use to ensure your media consumption supports your personal growth?

_____

_____

_____

_____

_____

What surprised you?

_____

_____

_____

_____

_____

_____

_____

_____

What upset you?

_____

_____

_____

_____

_____

_____

_____

_____

What was your biggest takeaway?

_____

_____

_____

_____

_____

_____

_____

Anything else worth noting:

_____

_____

_____

_____

_____

_____

_____

_____

What key takeaway will you highlight when you share this on social media (#SuccessMNSTR)?

_____

_____

_____

_____

_____

_____

_____

_____

P.S. Email the link to your post to Hello@SuccessMNSTR.com for an extra bonus!

Chapter 6
"N Stands for Neurochemical Understanding"

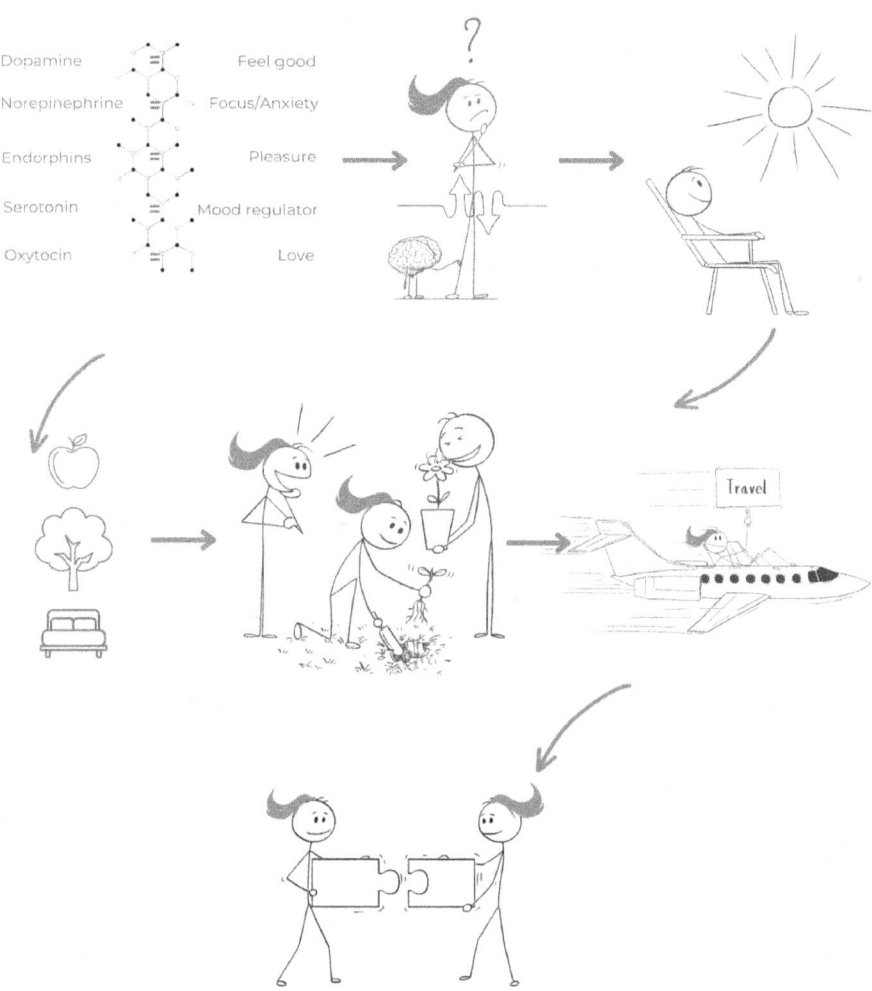

Dopamine	Feel good
Norepinephrine	Focus/Anxiety
Endorphins	Pleasure
Serotonin	Mood regulator
Oxytocin	Love

1. Related Questions with an Answer Key

Question: What role does dopamine play in success and motivation?

_____

_____

_____

_____

Answer: Dopamine acts as the "feel-good" neurotransmitter, significantly influencing motivation, pleasure, and positive reinforcement. It drives high achievers to pursue rewards and achievements but can also lead to overexertion.

Question: How does serotonin impact overall well-being?

_____

_____

_____

_____

_____

Answer: Serotonin regulates numerous brain functions and behaviors including mood, sleep, appetite, anger, and sexuality. Maintaining optimal levels stabilizes emotional fluctuations, fostering feelings of happiness and confidence.

Question: Describe how endorphins contribute to resilience.

_____

_____

_____

_____

_____

Answer: Endorphins are natural chemicals that alleviate pain, boost mood, and help individuals endure challenges. They are released during activities like exercise, enhancing the ability to persevere through difficult situations.

Question: What are the effects of norepinephrine on stress and alertness?

_____

_____

_____

_____

_____

Answer: Norepinephrine enhances alertness and reaction times during stressful situations. However, chronic high levels can lead to anxiety and burnout.

Question: Explain the importance of oxytocin in social bonding.

_____

_____

_____

_____

_____

Answer: Oxytocin, known as the "love hormone," regulates emotional connections and social bonding. It enhances feelings of trust and comfort in social interactions and helps maintain emotional well-being.

2. Multiple Choice Questions

Question: What neurotransmitter is primarily responsible for motivation and reward?

    a) Serotonin

    b) Norepinephrine

    c) Dopamine

    d) Endorphins

Answer: c) Dopamine

Question: Which neurotransmitter is linked to mood regulation and overall emotional balance?

    a) Dopamine

    b) Serotonin

    c) Norepinephrine

    d) Oxytocin

Answer: b) Serotonin

Question: What is the source of the "runner's high" that athletes feel after intense exercise?

    a) Dopamine

    b) Norepinephrine

    c) Endorphins

    d) Oxytocin

Answer: c) Endorphins

Question: Chronic stress and high levels of which neurotransmitter can lead to anxiety and burnout?

    a) Serotonin

    b) Oxytocin

    c) Endorphins

    d) Norepinephrine

Answer: d) Norepinephrine

Question: Which neurotransmitter is heavily involved in social bonding and emotional connections?

    a) Serotonin

    b) Oxytocin

    c) Dopamine

    d) Endorphins

Answer: b) Oxytocin

3. Topical Writing Prompts

Describe how understanding your own neurochemical processes can help you manage stress and increase productivity.

_____

_____

_____

_____

_____

_____

_____

_____

_____

Explain the significance of maintaining a balanced diet and regular exercise in regulating serotonin levels.

_____

_____

_____

_____

_____

_____

Discuss a personal experience where a surge of endorphins helped you overcome a challenging situation.

_____

_____

_____

_____

_____

Analyze the impact of oxytocin on your personal relationships and emotional well-being.

_____
_____
_____
_____
_____
_____

Reflect on a situation where heightened norepinephrine levels improved your performance during a stressful event.

_____
_____
_____
_____
_____
_____

4. Additional Workbook Activities

Matching Exercise:

Match the following terms with their definitions:

- a) Dopamine
- b) Serotonin
- c) Endorphins
- d) Norepinephrine
- e) Oxytocin

Definitions:

[iii] Plays a pivotal role in motivation and pleasure.

[ii] Regulates mood, sleep, and appetite.

[iv] Alleviate pain and boost mood during stress or physical activity.

[v] Enhances alertness and reaction times.

[i] Regulates social bonding and emotional connections.

Answer: a-iii, b-ii, c-iv, d-v, e-i

Fill-in-the-Blanks:

Complete the sentences with the correct words:

     1. Dopamine is often referred to as the "_____" neurotransmitter.

     2. Serotonin helps regulate mood, _____, and appetite.

     3. Activities such as exercise release _____, which alleviate pain and enhance mood.

     4. Norepinephrine plays a crucial role in the "_____" response, enhancing alertness.

     5. _____, often called the "love hormone," is important for social bonding.

Answer: feel-good, sleep, endorphins, fight-or-flight, Oxytocin

Discussion Topics:

Discuss the following topics in groups or pairs:

How can high achievers manage dopamine levels to avoid burnout?

_____

_____

_____

_____

_____

What lifestyle changes can people make to maintain optimal serotonin levels?

_____

_____

_____

_____

_____

In what ways do endorphins help individuals cope with physical and emotional stress?

_____

_____

_____

_____

_____

Explore the dual role of norepinephrine in enhancing focus and contributing to anxiety.

_____
_____
_____
_____
_____

How does oxytocin enhance the quality of personal and professional relationships?

_____
_____
_____
_____
_____

What surprised you?

_____
_____
_____
_____
_____
_____
_____
_____

What upset you?

_____
_____
_____
_____
_____
_____
_____
_____
_____

What was your biggest takeaway?

_____
_____
_____
_____
_____
_____
_____
_____

Anything else worth noting:

_____
_____
_____
_____
_____
_____
_____
_____
_____

What key takeaway will you highlight when you share this on social media (#SuccessMNSTR)?

_____
_____
_____
_____
_____
_____
_____
_____

P.S. Email the link to your post to Hello@SuccessMNSTR.com for an extra bonus!

Chapter 7
"S Stands for Satisfaction (Intrinsic vs. Extrinsic)"

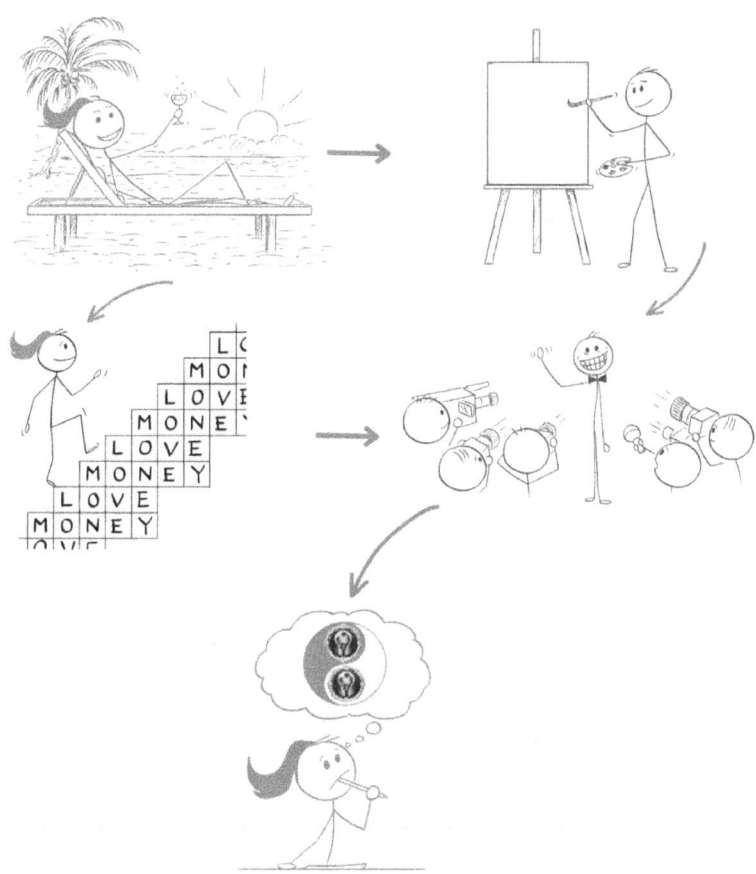

1. Related Questions with an Answer Key:

Question 1: Define intrinsic motivation and provide an example of it from the text.

_____

_____

_____

_____

Answer: Intrinsic motivation is driven by internal desires and passions rather than external rewards. For example, someone who loves painting does it for the joy and fulfillment in the process, not for awards or recognition.

Question 2: How does extrinsic motivation differ from intrinsic motivation?

_____

_____

_____

_____

Answer: Extrinsic motivation is driven by external rewards and recognition, such as financial incentives, social recognition, and material rewards, while intrinsic motivation is driven by internal satisfaction and personal values.

Question 3: Why is balancing intrinsic and extrinsic motivation important for sustainable success?

_____

_____

_____

_____

Answer: Balancing both types of motivation is crucial as intrinsic motivation ensures long-term engagement and personal fulfillment, while extrinsic motivation provides immediate positive reinforcement and direction. Together, they offer a comprehensive approach to achieving sustainable success.

Question 4: How can overemphasizing external rewards negatively impact intrinsic motivation?

_____

_____

_____

_____

Answer: Overemphasizing external rewards can overshadow internal drives, causing individuals to lose touch with their original passion and values, potentially diminishing their long-term satisfaction and engagement in their activities.

Question 5: What role does societal conditioning play in shaping our motivations?

_____

_____

_____

_____

Answer: Societal conditioning influences our values and aspirations by imposing cultural norms and expectations. These external pressures can steer us toward traditional milestones and careers, which may not always align with our true passions.

2. Multiple Choice Questions:

Question 1: What is the primary focus of intrinsic motivation?

    a) Financial rewards

    b) External recognition

    c) Personal values and joy of the process

    d) Achieving specific outcomes

Answer: c) Personal values and joy of the process

Question 2: Which of the following is an example of extrinsic motivation?

    a) Engaging in a hobby for the joy it brings

    b) Pursuing a degree out of genuine curiosity

    c) Working overtime to receive a bonus

    d) Learning a new language for personal fulfillment

Answer: c) Working overtime to receive a bonus

Question 3: How can intrinsic motivation benefit an individual when faced with challenges?

    a) By providing immediate rewards

    b) By offering external validation

    c) By driving perseverance due to passion

    d) By setting clear and attainable goals

Answer: c) By driving perseverance due to passion

Question 4: What is a potential downside of relying too much on extrinsic motivation?

    a) Immediate gratification

    b) Loss of internal drive

    c) Increased social recognition

    d) Enhanced personal growth

Answer: b) Loss of internal drive

Question 5: Which concept represents a harmonious balance between intrinsic and extrinsic motivations, as described in the book?

    a) Yin-yang symbol

    b) Carrot and stick

    c) Push and pull

    d) Reward and punishment

Answer: a) Yin-yang symbol

3. Topical Writing Prompts:

Describe a personal experience where intrinsic motivation played a crucial role in your achievement. How did this motivation help you persevere through challenges?

_____

_____

_____

_____

_____

_____

_____

_____

_____

_____

Analyze a situation where extrinsic motivation significantly influenced your actions. What were the outcomes, and how did the external rewards impact your drive?

_____

_____

_____

_____

_____

_____

_____

Reflect on a time when you had to balance both intrinsic and extrinsic motivations to achieve a goal. Discuss how you managed to maintain this balance.

_____

_____

_____

_____

_____

_____

Debate the statement: "In a world driven by external rewards, intrinsic motivation is becoming increasingly rare." Provide examples to support your argument.

_____

_____

_____

_____

_____

_____

Explore the societal expectations that have influenced your career or educational choices. How have you navigated these pressures to stay true to your passions?

_____

_____

_____

_____

_____

_____

4. Additional Workbook Activities:

Matching Exercise:

Match the following terms with their definitions:
- a) Intrinsic Motivation
- b) Extrinsic Motivation
- c) Personal Fulfillment
- d) External Rewards
- e) Societal Conditioning

Definitions:
1. Internal desires driving actions
2. Acknowledgement and tangible rewards from others
3. Cultural norms shaping aspirations
4. Satisfaction from aligning actions with personal values
5. Motivation stemming from outside incentives

Answers: a) 1 b) 5 c) 4 d) 2 e) 3

Fill-in-the-Blanks:

Complete the sentences with the correct words:

1. _____ is guided by internal desires, while _____depends on external rewards.
2. Someone who loves painting engages in it for the _____ and fulfillment it brings, not for _____ or recognition.
3. Balancing both _____ and _____ motivations is crucial for sustainable success.
4. Over-reliance on _____ rewards can diminish one's _____ drive.
5. Societal _____ often influences our choices and definitions of _____.

Answers: Intrinsic motivation, extrinsic motivation, joy, awards, intrinsic, extrinsic, external, internal, conditioning, success

Discussion Topics:

Discuss the following topics in groups or pairs:

How do you balance intrinsic and extrinsic motivations in your daily life?

_____

_____

_____

_____

_____

Share an example of a task you completed driven solely by intrinsic motivation. What was the outcome?

_____

_____

_____

_____

_____

Discuss the impact of societal pressures on career choices. Can you think of ways to resist these pressures?

_____

_____

_____

_____

_____

How can organizations create environments that nurture both intrinsic and extrinsic motivations among their employees?

_____

_____

_____

_____

_____

Reflect on a public figure who balances intrinsic and extrinsic motivations well. What lessons can we learn from their approach?

_____

_____

_____

_____

_____

What surprised you?

_____

_____

_____

_____

_____

_____

_____

_____

What upset you?

_____

_____

_____

_____

_____

_____

_____

_____

What was your biggest takeaway?

_____
_____
_____
_____
_____
_____
_____

Anything else worth noting:

_____
_____
_____
_____
_____
_____
_____

What key takeaway will you highlight when you share this on social media (#SuccessMNSTR)?

_____
_____
_____
_____
_____
_____
_____

P.S. Email the link to your post to Hello@SuccessMNSTR.com for an extra bonus!

Chapter 8
"T Stands for Treadmill Management (Hedonic)"

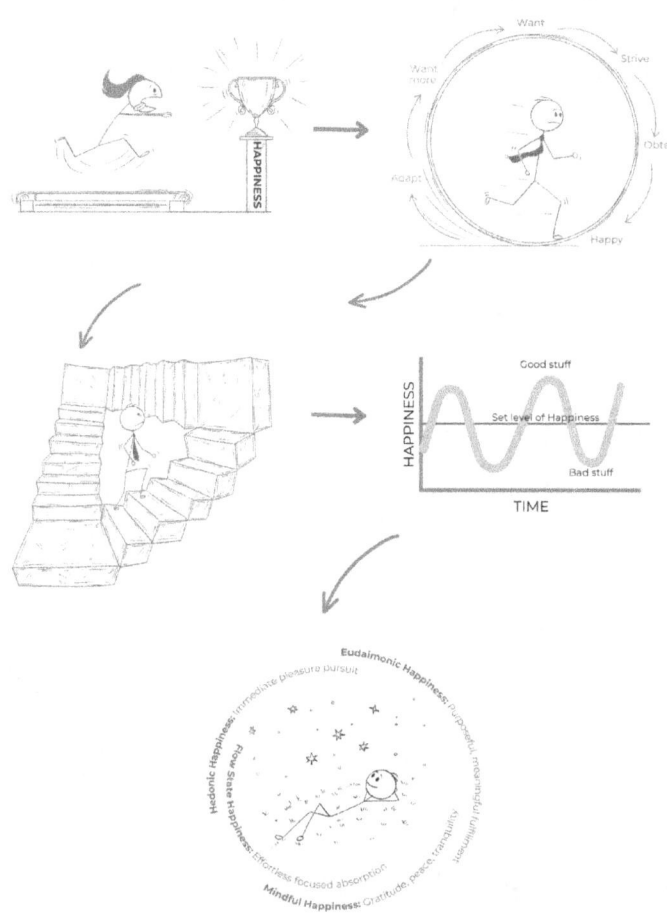

1. Related Questions with an Answer Key

Question: What is the hedonic treadmill, and how does it impact our pursuit of happiness?

_____

_____

_____

Answer: The hedonic treadmill is a psychological concept where individuals return to a stable level of happiness regardless of positive or negative events. This concept illustrates how obtaining new achievements or material possessions initially brings joy, but over time, that excitement diminishes, leading to a continuous cycle of seeking new accomplishments to maintain happiness.

Question: How can one cultivate mindfulness to cope with the hedonic treadmill?

_____

_____

_____

_____

Answer: Mindfulness can be cultivated through practices such as moments of reflection, body scanning, listening to music, meditation, creative arts, or journaling. These practices help individuals deeply appreciate the present moment, grounding them in their journey rather than the relentless pursuit of future achievements.

Question: What role do early life experiences play in shaping our happiness baseline?

_____

_____

_____

_____

Answer: Early life experiences significantly impact our emotional well-being. Attachments to caregivers, school experiences, and early friendships shape our emotional framework. Positive experiences and supportive relationships can strengthen emotional resilience, whereas adverse childhood experiences might affect emotional health into adulthood.

Question: Explain the four states of happiness mentioned in the chapter.

_____

_____

_____

_____

Answer: The four states of happiness are:
- *Hedonic Happiness: Derived from the pursuit of pleasure and avoidance of pain.*
- *Eudaimonic Happiness: Stemming from living a life of purpose and making a positive impact.*
- *Flow State Happiness: Achieved through total absorption in a challenging activity, leading to deep focus and enjoyment.*
- *Mindful Happiness: Rooted in appreciating small joys, finding beauty in the ordinary, and cultivating inner peace and tranquility.*

Question: How can fostering human connections help in escaping the hedonic treadmill?

_____

_____

_____

_____

Answer: Fostering human connections offers crucial support and reflects our values, which anchor us in what truly matters. Genuine connections help navigate life's challenges and offer a sense of belonging and validation, freeing us from the relentless pursuit of material or superficial forms of happiness.

2. Multiple Choice Questions

Question: What does the hedonic treadmill symbolize in the context of human psychology?

    a) Physical exercise

    b) Pursuit of steady income

    c) Continuous pursuit of happiness

    d) Balancing work and life

Answer: c) Continuous pursuit of happiness

Question: Which activity is NOT mentioned as a means to practice mindfulness?

    a) Meditation

    b) Body scanning

    c) Watching television

    d) Journaling

Answer: c) Watching television

Question: Which factor is NOT directly mentioned as influencing the happiness baseline?

    a) Genetic makeup

    b) Career achievements

    c) Early life experiences

    d) Personality traits

Answer: b) Career achievements

Question: According to Mihaly Csikszentmihalyi, what state is characterized by complete absorption in an activity?

    a) Eudaimonic state

    b) Flow state

    c) Mindful state

    d) Hedonic state

Answer: b) Flow state

Question: Which of the following is NOT a tool mentioned to help escape the hedonic treadmill?

    a) Embrace the present moment

    b) Align goals with societal expectations

    c) Celebrate simple joys

    d) Foster human connections

Answer: b) Align goals with societal expectations

3. Topical Writing Prompts

Discuss a time in your life when you felt caught in the hedonic treadmill. How did it affect your overall happiness and outlook on life?

_____
_____
_____
_____
_____
_____
_____
_____
_____
_____

Reflect on your current happiness baseline. What factors do you think have contributed most to it?

_____
_____
_____
_____
_____
_____
_____
_____

Describe an experience where you achieved flow state happiness. What were you doing, and how did it make you feel?

_____
_____
_____
_____
_____
_____
_____

How do you define success? Write about how your definition has changed over time.

_____

_____

_____

_____

_____

_____

Discuss the importance of human connections in your life. Provide examples of how they have helped you through challenging times.

_____

_____

_____

_____

_____

4. Additional Workbook Activities

Matching Exercise

Match the following terms with their definitions:
   a) Hedonic Happiness
   b) Eudaimonic Happiness
   c) Flow State Happiness
   d) Mindful Happiness
   e) Happiness Baseline
   c) Flow State Happiness

Definitions:
   1. Pursuit of pleasure and avoidance of pain.
   2. Pursuit of authenticity, meaning, virtue, and growth.
   3. Default level of contentment we return to after life's ups and downs.
   4. Complete absorption in a challenging activity.
   5. Ability to appreciate small joys and cultivate inner peace.
   6. Complete absorption in a challenging activity.

Answer: a-1, b-2, c-4, d-5, e-3, c-6

Fill-in-the-Blanks

Complete the sentences with the correct words:

1. The concept of the _____ treadmill explains how people continually strive for new achievements to maintain happiness.

2. _____ can be practiced through activities like meditation and journaling, helping individuals appreciate the present moment.

3. Early life experiences, such as _____ to caregivers, significantly impact our emotional well-being.

4. Achieving a _____ state involves deep focus and enjoyment in a challenging task.

5. Fostering human __ provides essential support and reflects values that anchor us in true happiness. (connections)

Answer: hedonic, Mindfulness, attachments, flow

Discussion Topics

Discuss the following topics in groups or pairs:

How can individuals break free from the hedonic treadmill in a consumer-driven society?

_____

_____

_____

_____

_____

What specific strategies can you employ to raise your happiness baseline?

_____

_____

_____

_____

_____

Share examples of hedonic and eudaimonic happiness in your life. How do they differ in terms of sustainability and depth?

_____

_____

_____

_____

_____

Discuss the role of mindfulness in achieving a balanced life. How can it be integrated into daily routines?

_____

_____

_____

_____

_____

Evaluate the importance of human connections in professional settings. How do they influence job satisfaction and overall happiness?

_____

_____

_____

_____

_____

What surprised you?

_____

_____

_____

_____

_____

_____

_____

What upset you?

_____

_____

_____

_____

_____

_____

_____

What was your biggest takeaway?

_____
_____
_____
_____
_____
_____
_____

Anything else worth noting:

_____
_____
_____
_____
_____
_____
_____

What key takeaway will you highlight when you share this on social media (#SuccessMNSTR)?

_____
_____
_____
_____
_____
_____
_____

P.S. Email the link to your post to Hello@SuccessMNSTR.com for an extra bonus!

Chapter 9
"R Stands for Restoration of Motivation and Wellness"

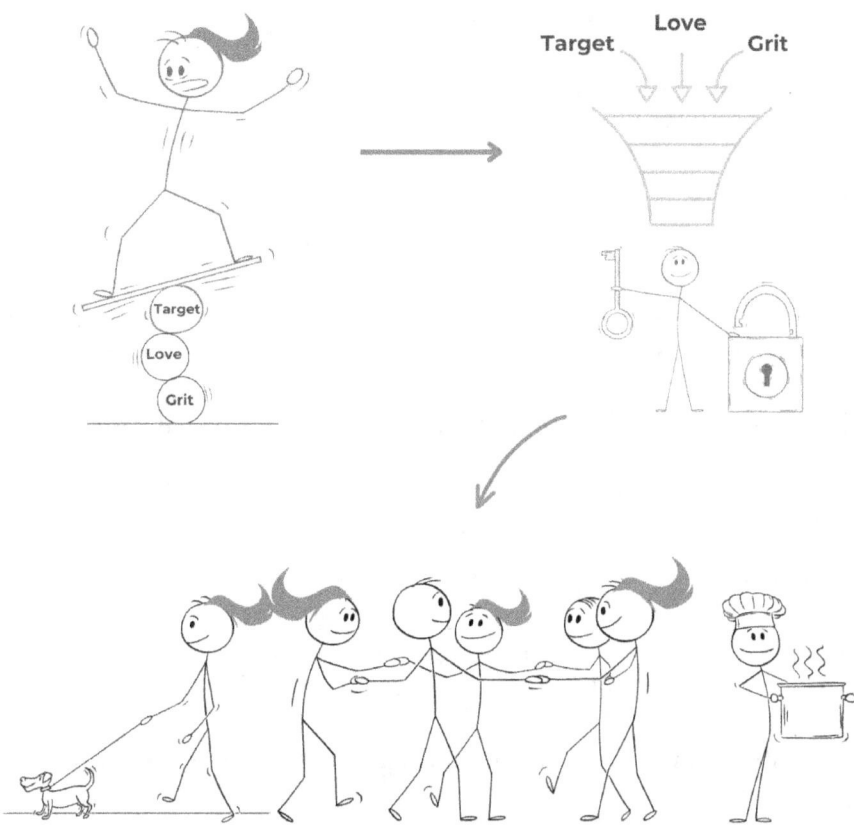

1. Related Questions with an Answer Key:

Question: What are the early signs of burnout, and how can one address them?

_____

_____

_____

_____

Answer: Early signs of burnout include feeling overwhelmed, postponing tasks, frequent illness, and emotional exhaustion. Addressing burnout involves recognizing these signs early, setting boundaries, adjusting workloads, and prioritizing well-being over perfection.

Question: What does it mean to find your "North Star," and why is it important?

_____

_____

_____

_____

Answer: Finding your "North Star" means discovering and aligning with your true passions and motivations. It is important because it helps maintain a sense of purpose and direction, preventing the feeling of running on a meaningless routine.

Question: How do flexible goals contribute to lasting motivation?

_____

_____

_____

_____

Answer: Flexible goals adapt to personal growth and changing circumstances, preventing disappointment and keeping the individual motivated. They allow for exploration and adaptation, ensuring that goals remain relevant and inspiring.

Question: Why is it important to have diverse interests, and how can this prevent burnout?

_____

_____

_____

_____

Answer: Having diverse interests keeps an individual energized and prevents the feeling of emptiness after completing a major goal. It ensures long-term enthusiasm and fulfillment by allowing engagement in various passions.

Question: What role does emotional and psychological resilience play in high achievement, and how can it be built?

_____

_____

_____

_____

Answer: Emotional and psychological resilience help manage stress and maintain mental clarity, essential for high achievement. It can be built through creative activities, physical challenges, and support groups, tailored to one's archetype and personal interests.

2. Multiple Choice Questions:

Question: What is a key factor in restoring motivation and wellness according to the chapter?

a) Ignoring stress

b) Recognizing early signs of burnout

c) Pushing through exhaustion

d) Abandoning goals frequently

Answer: b) Recognizing early signs of burnout

Question: Which of the following is NOT a recommended way to align with your North Star?

a) Ignoring your passions

b) Self-observation

c) Regularly reviewing your life choices

d) Aligning activities with your motivations

Answer: a) Ignoring your passions

Question: What is one benefit of setting flexible goals?

a) Ensuring rigid adherence to plans

b) Allowing for adaptability as circumstances change

c) Eliminating the need for planning

d) Preventing any form of disappointment

Answer: b) Allowing for adaptability as circumstances change

Question: How can embracing diverse interests benefit a high achiever?

a) By limiting their focus to one passion

b) By ensuring they never complete any project

c) By keeping them energized and preventing burnout

d) By avoiding any new challenges

Answer: c) By keeping them energized and preventing burnout

Question: According to the chapter, what key elements should be integrated into daily routines to maintain well-being?

a) Professional achievements and financial goals

b) Physical exercise, emotional practices, and social connections

c) Extensive work hours and limited sleep

d) Constant multitasking and avoidance of breaks

Answer: b) Physical exercise, emotional practices, and social connections

3. Topical Writing Prompts:

Reflect on a time when you experienced burnout. How did it affect different areas of your life, and what strategies did you implement to overcome it?

_____
_____
_____
_____
_____
_____
_____
_____
_____
_____
_____

Describe your "North Star" and how aligning with it has impacted your motivation and overall well-being.

_____
_____
_____
_____
_____
_____
_____

Discuss the importance of flexible goals in your life. Provide examples of how you have adapted your goals to stay motivated.

_____
_____
_____
_____
_____
_____

Explain the value of having diverse interests. How have you balanced your primary passion with other interests to maintain enthusiasm and prevent burnout?

_____

_____

_____

_____

_____

_____

Write about the strategies you use to build emotional and psychological resilience. How do these methods support your journey toward high achievement?

_____

_____

_____

_____

_____

_____

_____

4. Additional Workbook Activities:

Matching Exercise:

Match the following terms with their definitions:

   a) Burnout

   b) North Star

   c) Flexible Goals

   d) Psychological Resilience

   e) Spiritual Wellness

Definitions:

   1. True motivations guiding life choices.

   2. Deep emotional, mental, and physical exhaustion causing reduced productivity.

   3. Ability to manage stress and maintain mental clarity.

   4. Adaptable aspirations evolving with personal growth.

   5. Finding deeper meaning and connecting to a larger purpose.

Answer: a-2, b-1, d-3, c-4, e-5

Fill-in-the-Blanks:

Complete the sentences with the correct words:

1. Burnout is characterized by deep emotional, mental, and physical _____.
2. Aligning with your _____ helps maintain motivation and purpose.
3. Setting _____ goals allows for adaptation to personal growth and changing circumstances.
4. _____ ensures you remain engaged in various passions, preventing burnout.
5. Establishing routines that address physical, emotional, and _____ health is crucial for sustained motivation.

Answer: exhaustion, North Star, flexible, Diverse interests, spiritual

Discussion Topics:

Discuss the following topics in groups or pairs:

What are some early signs of burnout, and how can individuals proactively address them before they escalate?

_____
_____
_____
_____
_____

Share strategies for aligning daily activities with one's North Star. How can this alignment promote sustained motivation?

_____
_____
_____
_____
_____

Discuss the importance of flexible goals in a constantly changing world. How can personal growth impact goal setting?

_____
_____
_____
_____
_____

What are the benefits of having diverse interests, and how can high achievers balance focusing on a primary passion while exploring other interests?

_____

_____

_____

_____

_____

Explore ways to build emotional and psychological resilience through activities and community engagement. How do these strategies support high achievement?

_____

_____

_____

_____

_____

What surprised you?

_____

_____

_____

_____

_____

_____

_____

What upset you?

_____

_____

_____

_____

_____

_____

_____

What was your biggest takeaway?

_____
_____
_____
_____
_____
_____
_____
_____

Anything else worth noting:

_____
_____
_____
_____
_____
_____
_____
_____

What key takeaway will you highlight when you share this on social media (#SuccessMNSTR)?

_____
_____
_____
_____
_____
_____
_____

P.S. Email the link to your post to Hello@SuccessMNSTR.com for an extra bonus!

Chapter 10
The MNSTR Technique in Action

1. Related Questions with an Answer Key:

Question: What are the main challenges high achievers face according to "The MNSTR Technique in Action?"

_____

_____

_____

_____

Answer: High achievers often face depression, self-doubt, and identity crises due to the pressure of maintaining appearances and the emotional lows that follow their successes.

Question: Describe the MNSTR Technique and its purpose.

_____

_____

_____

_____

Answer: The MNSTR Technique is a framework that helps individuals overcome personal and professional challenges by focusing on Mindset, Neurochemical Understanding, Satisfaction, Treadmill Management, and Restoration of motivation and wellness.

Question: How did John use the MNSTR Technique to overcome his entrepreneurial struggles?

_____

_____

_____

_____

Answer: John used the MNSTR Technique by shifting his mindset, understanding his neurochemical responses, and restoring his motivation and wellness through exercise, healthy eating, and staying connected with loved ones.

Question: What did Lily learn about satisfaction, and how did it change her approach to art?

_____

_____

_____

_____

Answer: Lily learned to distinguish between intrinsic satisfaction (her love for creating art) and extrinsic validation (praise and likes). This understanding helped her focus on the pure joy of creation, transforming her artwork to convey raw emotion and truth.

Question: Explain David's transformation as a leader after implementing the MNSTR Technique.

_____

_____

_____

_____

Answer: David embraced neurochemical understanding, rediscovered his intrinsic values, and focused on self-restoration. This led him to infuse empathy and purpose into his leadership, making decisions that reflected human connections rather than just statistics.

2. Multiple Choice Questions:

Question: What is the primary goal of the MNSTR Technique?

    a) To achieve financial success

    b) To effectively break down personal challenges

    c) To gain approval from others

    d) To cultivate dependence on external validation

Answer: b) To effectively break down personal challenges

Question: In John's story, what did he do to regulate his neurochemicals?

    a) Increased his workload

    b) Focused on negative reminders

    c) Practiced gratitude and spent time in nature

    d) Avoided exercise and deep breathing

Answer: c) Practiced gratitude and spent time in nature

Question: How did Lily manage the cycle of emotional highs and lows?

    a) By quitting her art career

    b) By focusing only on external validation

    c) By curating media and social interactions

    d) By ignoring her core passions

Answer: c) By curating media and social interactions

Question: What realization helped David reconnect with his intrinsic values?

    a) Pursuing external rewards

    b) Exploring youthful passions

    c) Accumulating wealth

    d) Adhering to corporate rules

Answer: b) Exploring youthful passions

Question: What was the key to Sara's mindset transformation?

    a) Focusing solely on external recognition

    b) Discovering her core goals through old scrapbooks

    c) Ignoring her past achievements

    d) Chasing the next win perpetually

Answer: b) Discovering her core goals through old scrapbooks

3. Topical Writing Prompts:

Describe a time when you experienced a significant emotional low after a success. How could the MNSTR Technique have helped you navigate that period?

_____
_____
_____
_____
_____
_____
_____
_____
_____
_____

Reflect on an area of your life where you feel stuck. Choose one letter from the MNSTR acronym and explore how applying its principle could create change.

_____
_____
_____
_____
_____
_____

Write about a personal victory and the emotional aftermath. Using the MNSTR Technique, outline a plan to manage the neurochemical response to this event.

_____
_____
_____
_____
_____
_____

Consider a goal you achieved but felt disappointed afterward. Analyze why this happened and how the MNSTR Technique could help you redefine your satisfaction.

_____

_____

_____

_____

_____

_____

Describe a challenging period in your life. How might treadmill management and restoration of wellness principles assist you in handling similar situations in the future?

_____

_____

_____

_____

_____

4. Additional Workbook Activities:

Matching Exercise:

Match the following terms with their definitions:

    a) Mindset

    b) Neurochemical Understanding

    c) Intrinsic Satisfaction

    d) Hedonic Treadmill

    e) Restoration of Motivation and Wellness

Definitions:

1. The mental attitude that determines how you interpret and respond to situations.
2. Recognition and regulation of brain chemical responses to emotions and stress.
3. Finding joy in activities for their own sake rather than for external validation.
4. The tendency to pursue constant happiness through new achievements, leading to perpetual dissatisfaction.
5. Self-care practices that rejuvenate physical and emotional health.

Answer: a-1,b-2,c-3,d-4,e-5

Fill-in-the-Blanks:

Complete the sentences with the correct words:

1. John shifted his _____ from fixed to growth, viewing failures as feedback rather than dead ends.
2. Lily recognized the dangers of the _____ treadmil, switching her focus on her core passion.
3. David understood the importance of balancing neurochemicals like dopamine, serotonin, and _____ to maintain emotional well-being.
4. Sara created an "I did it list" as a portable reminder to reinforce her positive _____.
5. Alex prioritized her well-being by setting healthy _____ and focusing on self-reflection.

Answer: mindset, hedonic, norepinephrine, mindset, boundaries

Discussion Topics:

Discuss the following topics in groups or pairs:

How can the MNSTR Technique be applied to everyday challenges beyond professional success?

_____
_____
_____
_____
_____

Why is it important to distinguish between intrinsic and extrinsic satisfaction in achieving long-term happiness?

_____
_____
_____
_____
_____

Discuss the role of neurochemical understanding in managing stress and maintaining mental health.

_____
_____
_____
_____
_____

How can redefining success to include both highs and lows prepare individuals for future challenges?

_____

_____

_____

_____

_____

Explore the impact of the hedonic treadmill on high achievers and strategies to balance their ambition with self-care.

_____

_____

_____

_____

_____

MNSTR Technique: Where are you now? Quickly assess, pivot, and keep moving forward!

_____

_____

_____

_____

M: Mindset

1. Where's my head at right now?

_____

_____

_____

2. On a scale of 1 to 10, how is my mindset?

_____

_____

_____

3. What affected my mindset in that moment?

_____

_____

_____

_____

4. What could be contributing factors (stress, work, relationships)?

_____

_____

_____

_____

N: Neurochemical Balance

1. When was the last time I ate? Was it balanced?

_____

_____

_____

_____

2. Do I need a nap or rest?

_____

_____

_____

3. What does my body feel like when "mind drugs" (dopamine, etc.) are flowing?

_____

_____

_____

_____

4. Where do I physically feel these chemicals in my body?

_____

_____

_____

_____

S: Satisfaction (Intrinsic vs. Extrinsic)

1. Am I striving for something with no real meaning to me?

_____

_____

_____

_____

2. Is this goal aligned with my core values or is it externally driven?

_____

_____

_____

_____

3. Am I genuinely fulfilled by this pursuit?

_____

_____

_____

_____

4. What could I change to bring more satisfaction to this task?

_____

_____

_____

_____

T: Treadmill (Goal Management)

1. Am I chasing a goal that is too big or overwhelming right now?

_____

_____

_____

_____

2. How long have I been pushing without rest or recalibration?

_____

_____

_____

_____

3. Do I need to step off the treadmill and realign with something smaller or more meaningful?

_____

_____

_____

_____

4. Is this goal giving me joy or just pressure?

_____

_____

_____

_____

R: Restoration

1. Do I need to remove myself from this situation or environment to recharge?

_____

_____

_____

_____

2. Do I need space from a specific person or trigger?

_____

_____

_____

_____

3. What do I need at this moment (rest, food, a break)?

_____

_____

_____

_____

4. Can I identify a safe person to share this with?

_____

_____

_____

_____

5. Is there a peaceful place I can go to restore my energy?

_____

_____

_____

_____

What surprised you?

_____

_____

_____

_____

_____

_____

_____

What upset you?

_____

_____

_____

_____

_____

_____

What was your biggest takeaway?

_____

_____

_____

_____

_____

_____

Anything else worth noting:

_____

_____

_____

_____

_____

_____

What key takeaway will you highlight when you share this on social media (#SuccessMNSTR)?

_____

_____

_____

_____

_____

_____

P.S. Email the link to your post to Hello@SuccessMNSTR.com for an extra bonus!

Chapter 11
Harnessing your MNSTR: The Power Within

1. Related Questions with an Answer Key

Question 1: What role does naming your MNSTR play in establishing a connection with it?

_____

_____

_____

_____

Answer: Naming your MNSTR triggers a unique neurological response and creates an emotional bond, which deepens your relationship with your MNSTR.

Question 2: How can you leverage your MNSTR during times of conflict and challenge?

_____

_____

_____

_____

Answer: During times of anger or frustration, you should practice harnessing your MNSTR by realizing you have choices in how you react and respond. Achieving clarity often comes from allowing emotions to settle and sometimes acknowledging when you are wrong.

Question 3: What lesson can be learned from the story of the woman and the wine glasses?

_____

_____

_____

_____

Answer: The lesson is to focus intently on your goals and contributions, and not let others' disengagement affect your involvement. By concentrating on what you bring to the table, external distractions become irrelevant.

Question 4: According to the chapter, what spills from your cup during life's challenges?

_____

_____

_____

_____

Answer: What spills from your cup during life's challenges is whatever is inside you—whether it be joy, gratitude, peace, humility, or frustration, bitterness, and the urge to quit.

Question 5: What are the three key takeaways of this chapter?

_____

_____

_____

_____

Answer: The three key takeaways are: Name Your MNSTR to establish a deeper emotional connection, focus on what you can control by ignoring external distractions, and track and reflect daily to stay aligned with the MNSTR Technique.

2. Multiple Choice Questions

Question 1: What is the first step in harnessing your MNSTR?

a) Ignoring your MNSTR

b) Naming your MNSTR

c) Fighting your MNSTR

d) Denying your MNSTR

Answer: b) Naming your MNSTR

Question 2: In times of conflict, what is an essential practice according to the chapter?

a) Acting impulsively

b) Suppressing emotions

c) Harnessing your MNSTR

d) Distracting yourself

Answer: c) Harnessing your MNSTR

Question 3: What should you focus on to avoid external noise?

a) Other people's opinions

b) Your goals and contributions

c) External validation

d) Social media

Answer: b) Your goals and contributions

Question 4: When life shakes you, what spills over from your cup?

a) What you choose to put in it

b) External distractions

c) Other people's opinions

d) Nothing

Answer: a) What you choose to put in it

Question 5: What is required for achieving harmony within your MNSTR?

a) Ignoring your MNSTR

b) Daily self-awareness

c) Denying challenges

d) Giving up easily

Answer: b) Daily self-awareness

3. Topical Writing Prompts

Write about a situation where recognizing and naming your MNSTR helped you overcome a challenge. How did it change your perspective?

_____

_____

_____

_____

_____

_____

_____

_____

_____

_____

_____

Reflect on a recent conflict or frustration. How could you have harnessed your MNSTR to respond differently?

_____

_____

_____

_____

_____

_____

_____

Describe a scenario where you were distracted by external noise. How can you apply the lesson from the wine glass story to stay focused in similar situations?

_____

_____

_____

_____

_____

_____

_____

What do you usually spill from your cup when life gets tough? How can you work on filling your cup with positive attributes?

_____

_____

_____

_____

_____

_____

How do you plan to implement daily self-reflection to stay aligned with the MNSTR Technique?

_____

_____

_____

_____

_____

_____

4. Additional Workbook Activities

Matching Exercise:

Match the following terms with their definitions:
- a) MNSTR.
- b) Self-Reflection
- c) External Noise
- d) Clarity
- e) Resilience

Definitions:

1. The ability to recover quickly from setbacks.
2. A personal motivator and cheerleader inside you.
3. Regularly assessing and reflecting on your actions and thoughts.
4. Understanding your emotions and responses after allowing time for emotions to settle.
5. Distractions and opinions from others that can affect your focus.

Answer: e-1, a-2, b-3, d-4, c-5

Fill-in-the-Blanks:

Complete the sentences with the correct words:

1. Naming your MNSTR creates an emotional bond and triggers a unique neurological _____.

2. During times of conflict, practicing harnessing your MNSTR helps you realize that you have _____ in how you react.

3. The lesson from the wine glass story is to focus intently on your goals and _____.

4. When life shakes you, it's what's _____ you that spills over.

5. Daily self-awareness is essential for achieving ____ within your MNSTR.

Answer: response, choices, contributions, inside, harmony

Discussion Topics:

Discuss the following topics in groups or pairs:

How does naming your MNSTR influence your personal growth?

_____

_____

_____

_____

_____

Share a challenging moment where you could have better harnessed your MNSTR. What would you do differently now?

_____

_____

_____

_____

_____

Discuss the importance of focusing on your own goals and contributions rather than external distractions.

_____

_____

_____

_____

_____

What does the concept of "what's in your cup" mean to you? How can you apply it to your everyday life?

_____
_____
_____
_____
_____

How can the daily practice of self-reflection benefit your personal and professional life?

_____
_____
_____
_____
_____

What surprised you?

_____
_____
_____
_____
_____
_____
_____
_____

What upset you?

_____
_____
_____
_____
_____
_____
_____
_____

What was your biggest takeaway?

_____

_____

_____

_____

_____

_____

_____

Anything else worth noting:

_____

_____

_____

_____

_____

_____

_____

What key takeaway will you highlight when you share this on social media (#SuccessMNSTR)?

_____

_____

_____

_____

_____

_____

_____

P.S. Email the link to your post to Hello@SuccessMNSTR.com for an extra bonus!

Chapter 12
Navigating Your Cycles of Sabotage or Comfort

1. Related Questions with an Answer Key:

Question 1: What is the main purpose of the Success Paradox Self-Assessment as described in the chapter?

_____

_____

_____

_____

Answer: The main purpose of the Success Paradox Self-Assessment is to help individuals identify and understand their cycles of self-sabotage and comfort, particularly after achieving goals, in order to take control of their personal growth and overcome obstacles that hinder their progress.

Question 2: How is success redefined in this chapter beyond traditional measures?

_____

_____

_____

_____

Answer: Success is redefined as a journey marked by internal revelations, hard-won lessons, and deeper insights rather than just surface-level accomplishments. It involves finding a balance between achievement and inner fulfillment.

Question 3: According to the chapter, what are some common patterns of self-sabotage that individuals might face?

_____

_____

_____

_____

Answer: Common patterns of self-sabotage include perfectionism, lack of trust, fear of failure, imposter syndrome, the need for validation, and feelings of never being happy or good enough.

Question 4: What are the dual aspects of the Success MNSTR Archetype emphasized in the chapter?

_____

_____

_____

_____

Answer: The dual aspects are the "Light Side" (positive behaviors such as savoring success, self-awareness, self-clarity, self-expression, and self-release) and the "Dark Side" (negative behaviors such as sabotaging success, self-doubt, active avoidance, censorship, and harsh criticism).

Question 5: How does Simone Biles' story illustrate the core message of the chapter?

_____

_____

_____

_____

Answer: Simone Biles' story illustrates that true greatness and success come from honoring one's well-being and finding a balance between ambition and health. Her decision to prioritize her mental health over titles reflects embracing one's personal limits and managing the Success MNSTR.

2. Multiple Choice Questions:

Question 1: What is the Success Paradox Self-Assessment designed to help you recognize?

    a) Your physical fitness levels

    b) Your financial stability

    c) Your cycles of self-sabotage and comfort

    d) Your social relationships

Answer: c) Your cycles of self-sabotage and comfort

Question 2: Which of the following is NOT a component of the Success MNSTR Technique?

a) Mindset

b) Neurochemical

c) Strategy

d) Restoration

Answer: c) Strategy

Question 3: What should you do after noticing cycles of sabotage according to the chapter?

a) Ignore them and move on

b) Reflect and take the self-assessment again

c) Take control and address them for future growth

d) Celebrate and rest

Answer: c) Take control and address them for future growth

Question 4: What kind of balance is essential for maintaining motivation after reaching milestones?

a) Balance between work and leisure

b) Balance between achievement and inner fulfillment

c) Balance between diet and exercise

d) Balance between financial and social aspects

Answer: b) Balance between achievement and inner fulfillment

Question 5: What is an example of a Success MNSTR leading to self-doubt after an accomplishment?

a) Feeling overjoyed

b) Experiencing imposter syndrome

c) Celebrating continuously

d) Setting new goals immediately

Answer: b) Experiencing imposter syndrome

3. Topical Writing Prompts:

Write about a time when you achieved a significant goal but felt a sense of let-down afterward. How did you handle your feelings?

_____

_____

_____

_____

_____

_____

_____

_____

_____

_____

Describe your understanding of the Success MNSTR and how it impacts both your personal and professional life.

_____

_____

_____

_____

_____

_____

_____

Reflect on a moment when self-sabotage hindered your progress. What were the triggers, and how did you cope with them?

_____

_____

_____

_____

_____

_____

Discuss the importance of balancing achievement with inner fulfillment based on examples from people you admire, such as Simone Biles.

_____

_____

_____

_____

_____

_____

How can regularly using tools like the Success Paradox Self-Assessment contribute to your long-term personal growth?

_____

_____

_____

_____

_____

_____

4. Additional Workbook Activities:

Matching Exercise:

Match the following terms with their definitions:

   a) Self-Awareness

   b) Perfectionism

   c) Imposter Syndrome

   d) Self-Reflection

   e) Balance

Definitions:

   1. An even distribution of aspects of life to maintain stability and well-being

   2. The process of contemplating one's thoughts, feelings, and actions for growth

   3. Feeling undeserving of success and fearing exposure as a fraud

   4. The need for everything to be flawless, often hindering progress

   5. Recognizing and understanding one's own behaviors and emotions

Answer: e-1, d-2, c-3, b-4, a-5

Fill-in-the-Blanks:

Complete the sentences with the correct words:

1. The Success Paradox Self-Assessment helps you identify cycles of _____ and _____.

2. Simone Biles prioritized her _____ over reclaiming titles, illustrating her mastery of balancing ambition and well-being.

3. Success is not a one-size-fits-all formula but involves internal _____ and continuous growth.

4. Regular _____ is essential to breaking limiting patterns and pursuing meaningful success.

   5. Recognizing the _____ side of your Success MNSTR can help you address negative behaviors that hinder progress.

Answer: Sabotage, Comfort, Health, Revelations, Self-reflection, Dark

Discussion Topics:

Discuss the following topics in groups or pairs:

Share your experiences of self-sabotage and how they have affected your achievements.

_____

_____

_____

_____

_____

Debate the importance of mental health in achieving success and cite examples like Simone Biles.

_____

_____

_____

_____

_____

Discuss how self-awareness and self-reflection can lead to personal and professional growth.

_____

_____

_____

_____

_____

Explore ways to challenge comfort zones and set adaptive goals for continuous improvement.

_____

_____

_____

_____

_____

Reflect on the role of honest self-assessment in overcoming impostor syndrome and building self-confidence.

_____

_____

_____

_____

_____

What surprised you?

_____

_____

_____

_____

_____

_____

What upset you?

_____

_____

_____

_____

_____

_____

_____

What was your biggest takeaway?

_____
_____
_____
_____
_____
_____
_____

Anything else worth noting:

_____
_____
_____
_____
_____
_____
_____

What key takeaway will you highlight when you share this on social media (#SuccessMNSTR)?

_____
_____
_____
_____
_____
_____
_____

Who will you refer the Success MNSTR book to and why?

Name:

_____

_____

Date:

_____

_____

Why should they read it?

_____

_____

_____

_____

_____

What date will you discuss each others findings?

_____

_____

Have you shared your #Success MNSTR with the world yet?

Do any of your friends have the same Archetype as you?

Post and you may be pleasantly surprised 😊

_____

_____

_____

_____

_____

_____

_____

Thank You

Thank you for taking the time to read my book and for diving deep into your own self-discovery.

Here's to mastering your Success MNSTR and achieving everything you want in this one beautiful life we get!

Scan the QR Code with your phone or type in the URL to access the online resources:

www.successmnstr.com/resources

www.ingramcontent.com/pod-product-compliance
Lightning Source LLC
Chambersburg PA
CBHW081001120626
46546CB00010B/2992